Preparing for Jesus

The story of Jesus' birth,
based on Matthew 2:1–12
and Luke 2:1–21, for children.

Written by Lisa M. Clark
Illustrated by David Miles

CONCORDIA PUBLISHING HOUSE • SAINT LOUIS

Time to get ready! Yes, time to prepare:
We've got a beautiful message to share!
We know the Savior came down from His throne,
Keeping His promise to make us His own!

Born as a baby, His very first bed
Was in a manger, where cattle were fed!
Humble and lowly, He slept on the hay;
Perfect and holy, our debts He would pay.

Creatures surrounded the almighty King;
Heaven and nature all gathered to sing
There in a town by the prophets foreseen.
Oh, what a message! And oh, what a scene!

Bright in the sky, angels hovered above,
Telling some shepherds of God's precious love:
"Glory to God and His peace on this night;
Go see the One who will make all things right!"

At the same time, Wise Men found a great star
Shining the news of a wonder afar:
God sent the light of the world to the earth.
Oh, what a message! And oh, what a birth!

Both God and man, Jesus' mission to save
Led to the trials, the cross, and the grave.
There in a garden, our Savior would rise,
Giving us life as an Easter surprise!

Angels were there to proclaim the Good News:
Jesus has won and the devil would lose!
Christ would return, ev'ry sin to destroy:
Oh, what a message! And oh, what a joy!

Jesus, our Savior, will one day return.

Now we get ready and help others learn:

When He comes back, He will make all things new!

Let's share the message in all that we do!

Dear Family,

When Jesus was born, there were many messengers to tell the Good News! Angels told the shepherds, and the shepherds told others. A special star and the Scriptures told the Wise Men, and the Wise Men told others too. Later, angels told the women at the tomb that Jesus rose from the dead, and they shared the news with others!

We know the Good News of Jesus. We know that He came to be born as a baby. We know that He taught and healed. We know that He died and rose. We know that He saves us from sin and death. We know that He promises to return and make everything perfect again. Now, it's our turn to tell others!

Christmas gives us many opportunities to tell about Jesus. We can share the Good News in the cards we send, in the ways we care, and in the songs we sing. Even our decorations can help us think about Jesus! What do your family decorations teach about the Son of God, the Savior of the world?

Blessings to you and your family as you share the love of Jesus with others and with one another.

The Author